The Little Book of

Flash Fiction

Super short stories,

playful and poetic, strange and dark

including 100-word drabbles and

150-word micro fiction

The Little Book of Flash Fiction
Playful Poetic Strange Dark - All Super Short

The Small Print

ISBN: 978-0-9878178-6-0

Written and published by Patricia Timmermans

Printed by Amazon KDP

July 2025

Thank you for supporting independent creators.

❖   ❖   ❖

Table of Contents

The Little Book of Flash Fiction
Playful Poetic Strange Dark - All Super Short

Author's note

The Little Book of Flash Fiction is a collection of ultra-short stories; each one told in less than 150 words.

They're funny, poetic, sincere and some are dark. Each story invites you to experience a full narrative arc in the time it takes to brew your morning coffee.

This collection is a celebration of language, brevity, and the joy of storytelling.

Why I wrote these stories

I wrote these pieces for a flash fiction and drabble challenge. A drabble is a story told in exactly 100 words, and flash fiction covers super short or micro fiction. Each must be a complete story.

Today I've collected and dusted them off to publish in this little book. Why? Because they should be shared.

I hope you enjoy reading them as much as I loved writing them!

Sincerely,

Patricia Timmermans

1.

Pets with Personality

This chapter features guide dog Cooper, with Buddy and Zoey the cats.

You'll recognize Cooper and his cat housemates from
Dear Diary Love Cooper

These three have lots of stories to tell, and I (the ghostwriter) love telling them.

I hope you enjoy these clips from their (our) lives.

Two Cats and the Dog Talk Soaps

A 100-word story using the word "married"

"If that darn bird would just shut up, I could watch my show!" complained Zoey.

"I ate birds when I was an alley boss," Buddy bragged, "Want me to eat him?"

Zoey looked disgusted, "What do they taste like?"

"Chicken."

"That's a stretch," Cooper added sarcastically.

"Yes, eat the bird," Zoey said, "I've been waiting for this part — Nikki and Victor are getting married."

"You're not missing anything," said Buddy. "It's the third time they're tying the knot."

"How do you know, tough guy?"

"I watched soaps through people's windows."

Zoey smiled at Buddy dreamily, "You're a soft old boss."

Why Does She Always Suspect Us?

A 100-word story using the word "broken"

On an ordinary day, all is quiet until a ceramic vase crashes to the floor.

The lady: Hey, you three, it looks like something is broken…

Buddy: Her powers of observation are remarkable.

Zoey: That sounds like an accusation. Maybe it fell on its own, why are we the suspects?

Buddy: We're the only ones here! And things don't just fall on their own.

Zoey: The only movement in this room was the dog, walking around and wagging his tail.

Cooper: Who me? I didn't see anything.

Buddy: Do you look behind you while you're walking past the coffee table?

Feline Antics

A 100-word story using the word "feline"

"Today's word is *feline* and I know what the lady will write," explained Buddy.

"What, pray tell me, sagely, wise one?" Zoey asked.

"Feline antics," Buddy nodded, appreciative of being acknowledged accurately.

"How do you know?"

"I was reading over her shoulder. The story on her phone said *feline*, then I heard her say, *I'll write about feline antics*."

"Good point," Zoey gave him that. "You know what I read over her shoulder?"

"You can read?" Buddy lifted an eyebrow.

"50 exercises for cats — and we know who here needs exercise."

"That's why there's catnip in my toy," Buddy muttered.

A True Master

A 100-word drabble using the word "historian"
including an original haiku

"The lady and I visited the library yesterday;
we saw Beatrice," Cooper told Zoey.

"Who's Beatrice?" Zoey asked.

"The historian who works there, she is also
a haiku master."

"A what master?"

"Haiku — a short poem of three lines, often of
beauty and nature."

"I thought it was a sneeze," Zoey grinned.

"Nope, listen to this one,

My words are daisies
I whisper them to your heart
You see with your heart

"I heard Beatrice reciting it to a little blind
girl."

Zoey dabbed a tear from her face and mewed,
"That was beautiful, she is a true haiku master."

Alcohol-free Water for the Navigator

A 100-word story using the word "alcohol"

"Hey, Cooper, where were you and the lady?" Zoey asked.

"The casino, she says I'm her lucky charm," Cooper replied.

Zoey waited, listening closely.

Cooper went on, "She said if I found a lucky seat, we'd celebrate with BLTs, no lettuce or tomatoes on mine."

"You're spoiled," Zoey sighed.

"I'm as dependable as ants at a picnic."

"What does that even mean?" Zoey looked confused.

"I found her a seat.

"She sat down, ordered me an alcohol-free water, pulled the lever, got sevens, bells clanged, we cashed out, and voila!

"A BLT with only bacon. She's *my* lucky charm!"

Why Dogs Don't Swim in Kids Pools

A 100-word story using the word "observed"

One scorching afternoon, Pat said, in her overly encouraging voice, "Go ahead Cooper, jump into the pool, it's okay your feet are clean."

I wasn't worried about my feet!

I was suspicious of the child. He was in there for a while with no bathroom breaks.

Eventually, I stepped in, but I was not happy, and labs love water. What I don't do in the name of harmony.

Pat observed the situation and sensed I wasn't happy, so she handed me some bacon treats.

Sweet! I thought. Just look unimpressed, stare into the distance, and — success! Delicious bacon every time.

Dogs Are Spiritual, Cats Think They Are

A 100-word story using the word "spiritual" and the phrase "The colour tasted like watermelon."

"Hey, Cooper," Buddy asked, looking thoughtful, "Are dogs spiritual?"

"Absolutely," Cooper replied, "Sirius, the Dog Star, is the brightest in the night sky. It shines on me and blesses my life."

"I thought Sirius was a radio station," Zoey chimed in.

Buddy rolled his eyes and said, "Did you know Leo, the most famous cosmic cat, is a constellation and the fifth sign of the Zodiac."

Zoey, looking smug, added, "Did you guys know the star signs have colours, and one of Leo's colours is red?"

Cooper and Buddy's jaws dropped.

"I dreamed about it. The colour tasted like watermelon."

Things Cats Will and Will Not Admit

A 100-word story using the word "loath" and phrase "thunderous sounds filled…"

"Hey Cooper," asked Buddy, "You know Zoey is loath to admit she loves us?"

Cooper, looking confused, said, "Isn't *loath* a chunk of bread people slice for sandwiches?"

"That's a loaf, old chap, sliced for toast."

Just then, thunderous sounds filled the hall as Zoey sprinted down the stairs.

"I thought I heard my name used in a phrase with *loaf* — I'm no loaf."

"It was *loath*," Buddy explained, "About how you won't admit things."

"Like what?" Zoey asked.

"Like your love for sandwiches," Cooper grinned.

"I'm loath to admit anything," Zoey agreed, "Except how much I love you guys."

Who's Smarter - Dogs, Cats, or Buddy?

A 150-word story using the word "family"

"Have you noticed dogs are always tethered to a human with a leash?" Zoey asked.

"That's because cats are smarter, we'd survive out there. I would anyway, but dogs would not," Buddy boasted.

"Excuse me, who always gets what she wants? I mew sweetly and, voila!"

"Sure, but did you survive in the alleys eating scraps; getting chased by coyotes and children?"

"Perhaps not, but I wore a pitiful face, got dropped into a box and when they opened it, I was part of this family."

"Have you tried leaving?"

"Once, I dashed outside and up a tree. I saw everything from up there!"

"Your point?"

"If I get lost, I'll dash up a tree."

"How did you get back inside?"

"The lady coaxed me with canned chicken."

"You fell for that old trick?"

"Nope, I held out for chicken with gravy."

"Indeed, we are both equally smart," Buddy agreed.

Cats Are Sophisticated

A 100-word story using the word "torrent"; the first and last sentences are the same

The thunder continued to roll.

"Hey, Cooper," Buddy asked, "Why do you run downstairs when it rains?"

"Only when rain falls in a torrent," Cooper replied.

Buddy, believing cats are superior, said, "You ought to, more correctly, say, I leave when the rain is torrential."

"You're saying your way is more correct?" Cooper asked, "That would imply my way is also correct, and who says *ought* anymore?"

"Cats, they're more sophisticated than dogs," Buddy bragged.

"You guys ought to relax," Zoey chimed in. "The Weather Network predicts a new torrent's coming."

Buddy and Cooper blinked.

The thunder continued to roll.

The Weird Wee Hours

A 100-word story using the word "wraith"

"I wandered down to the kitchen in the wee hours and saw the weirdest thing," Buddy told Cooper.

"Everything is weird in the wee hours," Cooper nodded.

"At a glance, I thought it was a wraith."

"What's a wraith?"

"They're wispy things, the humans' name for underweight ghosts."

"What was it?"

"Sheer curtains on the big window, but that's not all."

"Mmm hmm?" Cooper hummed, still listening.

"From the tabletop, I glanced next door and saw George chowing down on a donut."

"What's weird about that?"

"George is dead."

Cooper nodded, "I understand completely. George comes back for the donuts."

The Dog Guest

A 150-word story using the word "stick"

"Cooper, what's got you down?" asked Buddy.

"I need Solo to go home," Cooper complained.

"He's taking liberties."

"Liberties?" Buddy seemed concerned.

"He drools in my water dish, which grosses me out."

Buddy shuddered.

"He snags my round dog bed, leaving me the square one."

Buddy nodded. "He spins ten times before lying down, he'd fall off the square one."

"Good point," Cooper agreed, "and he buried my femur underground, behind the shed."

Buddy gasped. "There's got to be a limit."

"Who's underground?" Zoey chimed in.

"No one," sighed Buddy. "I'll get the femur. I've got connections on the outside."

"You mean the stick I saw Solo burying this morning?"

They both stared at Zoey.

She continued, "Your femur is under the square bed, Cooper. I shoved it under your bed when Solo was outside."

"You guys are the best."

"We are," both cats agreed. "We've got your back, Cooper."

Was it Connie and Fred?

(The silliest story ever)

A 100-word story with the word "sight" in a limerick

> *On Thursday, a dog and a cat,*
> *Discussing their lives and all that,*
> *They first saw bright eyes,*
> *Against the night skies,*
> *When suddenly, in flew a bat.*

"What now?" asked Cooper.

Buddy was scratching his head.

The bat circled, and, in a perfect British accent, said "If you please, I'm looking for Connie and Fred."

Buddy said, "Am I right, bats don't need sight in the dark? If so, check the park, they're hanging about with a lark."

"Hey Bud, you figure that was Connie and Fred in the tree?"

"Who can tell? All bats look alike to me."

Buddy's Deal With the Dog

A 100-word story using the word "closely"

They were meant to be forgotten, those horrid dog socks.

"What's got you down big guy?" Buddy asked.

"I dropped my dog socks into the bin, and they're back," Cooper sighed.

"The lady is probably thinking ahead to winter."

"I'm descended from the mighty timber wolf," Cooper explained, "Have you seen the lord of the frozen wilderness wearing red socks?"

Buddy grinned, "See these claws, Cooper?"

Cooper looked closely.

They make the ninja salad chopper seem like a kitten's toy, and I'll need extra stuffing in your cushion, the one I borrow."

"You've got a deal, Buddy, you're the best!"

More Buddy stories in Chapter 7 Buddy's Bravado

2.

Prose Like Poetry

These playful and lyrical stories are written as poems, and each one is exactly100 words.

Don't Forget, Get Laid

A 100-word story, including the word "laid"

When I set books down on the desk, I don't say *lie* but *lay,*

If I had set them yesterday, it's *laid*, and never *layed*.

So, who came up with *'layed'?* I asked the wise ones on the net.

An error some will make, they said, seems tenses they don't get.

Remember people lying lie, and books on desks are laid,

To *lay* is now, *lie down* is too, it's *'layed'* we should evade.

I need to rest my mind, now on my soft couch I will *lay*,

But wait! It's *lie* to rest right now, and *laid* was yesterday.

White Angel vs. Devil Boy

A 100-word story, including the word "work"

"Get up, let's get to work," White Angel on my shoulder said.

"Who needs the stress," Red Devil asked, "why not just stay in bed?"

"She's not that stressed," White Angel said, "no need to waste the day.

"She loves her job, so does the dog, God knows they're weird that way.

"Their path winds through the park, it's pleasant even in the rain."

"Heck, rain's no fun," said Devil Boy, "it's soggy bleak and grim."

"Be quiet guys! Enough," I said. "It might be bleak and grim.

"But I don't care, it's Saturday, we're all going to the gym."

We're Almost Eight

A 100-word story, including the word "almost"

Now we're just two it's you and me
In two short weeks, we will be three.

We three and possibly one more
I'm sure we'll have the room for four.

On second thought we'd feel alive
Us three, two pups, a perfect five.

Think of the fun if we were six,
Six beating hearts, a perfect mix.

I'm thinking it would be like heaven
Us three, four pups would make us seven.

Four pups will soon become four dogs
They'll play and romp and jump like frogs.

The shelter's near we're almost late
Let's go real quick before we're eight.

Signed By the Cat

A 100-word poem, including the word "surprise"

The cats slept on the sofa, and
the dog snored on the floor,

The doorbell rang, they all looked up,
who could be at the door?

The postman called from on the porch,
A signature I'll need.

So, Buddy dipped his claw in ink,
said, *this should do indeed.*

*I sign for parcels when she's gone,
she says I'm worth her trust.*

The postman, shocked and quite surprised,
said, *sign here if you must.*

The cats and Cooper laughed so hard,
they all fell on the floor,

They won't believe him when he says,
a cat signed at the door.

This Aging Thing is Not My Bag

A 100-word story using the word "scientist"

I asked the Doc, "What's going on? I'm up too late, and all day I yawn.

"My knees both creak, my hair is thin, I yank small whiskers from my chin."

The Doc said, "You're smart, you'll get the gist, it shouldn't take a scientist.

"So, stretch each day and ride your bike, on weekends you could take a hike."

Agreed, the Doc is usually right, my fitness plans begin tonight.

I'll eat my spinach, skip the kale, from yoga class, I'll try not to bale.

I can't become a cranky hag, but this aging thing is not my bag.

3.

A Hint at Horror

These short tales are eerie, unsettling, and darkly satisfying.

In just a few words, they offer enough to send a chill down your spine, maybe make you glance over your shoulder.

A Monster at the Gate

A 100-word story, including the word "face"

I heard frantic pounding, followed by screams.
It was Pam, and on her face — pure terror.

"Where's your key and what is that?" I yelled,
throwing open the door.

Outside the gate: snarling, vicious and wet. I
glimpsed enormous, bloody fangs.

"It's getting in!" Pam cried.

She clambered inside as our wolfdog,
Stealthmode, dashed past, out the door and flew
across the yard.

She leapt the gate and seconds later, silence.

"Stealth?" I called, hopefully.

Instantly she appeared at our sides, wagging her
tail.

We embraced our hero, collapsing into her fur,
We desperately missed our home, back on
Earth.

The Trapdoor

A 100-word story, including the word "blast"

Like a shotgun blast, a thunderclap pierced the dark night, and lightning lit up the forest floor.

Pounding footsteps grew louder, closer. Finally, I spotted it – the trapdoor! I'd climb in and lock it from inside.

I eased it open hoping he wouldn't hear its rusty hinges creak. But instead of slipping inside, I ducked to the side, leaving a gaping hole between us.

In the blackness, my stalker didn't see the hole and tumbled in.

I slammed the trapdoor shut, jammed a branch through the latch, and prayed it would hold.

Then I ran.

I ran for my life.

Ice Water or Maybe Something Stronger?

A 100-word story, including the word "classic"

The sounds of music boxes once soothed me, particularly when I was a child.

I adored the tiny chimes often playing lullabies, until I made the mistake of watching the classic horror, *Rosemary's Baby.*

My dread over music boxes was equal to, possibly greater than, my fear of clowns.

On Christmas morning of 2010, a mysterious ornament appeared under the tree.

"What an adorable little painted box," I murmured, and began turning the crank on its side.

"Is this a jack-in-the…?"

Some time later I awoke to my sister offering me ice water and aspirins.

Instead, I poured a whisky.

4.

Didn't See That Coming

These short stories take a turn when you least expect it.

Each one is under 150 words and will keep you guessing right to the final line.

The Dusty Old Violin Case

A 100-word story, including the word "rapid"

"I'm not going to the reading of the will," Marian insisted. "Thirty years ago, she wrote me off. I don't care about her stuff."

The lawyer assured Marian there would be no conflicts, after all, her mother was dead.

"Good point," Marian relented.

Marian felt her rapid heartbeat in her chest when, after the reading, the lawyer handed her a dusty old violin case.

That case had remained under Marian's bed when she left home.

"So what about it?" Marian shrugged.

The lawyer asked Marian to Google three words: *pristine, original*, and *Stradivarius*.

Marian turned white. Then she fainted.

Finally, the Letter

A 100-word story including the word "coast"

"Mom please, hand me the letter," Pammy's heart pounded in her throat as she spoke.

Her mother whispered, "Why is he still writing to you?"

"He loves me, Mom. My flight is booked, and I'm leaving tomorrow for the coast."

Her mother brushed past Pammy, paused as if to speak but left, and the door gently clicked shut behind her, which was more disturbing than if she'd slammed it.

Pammy snapped up the letter her mother had dropped and tore it open.

The words blurred and her knees buckled beneath her as she read,

My heart breaks to write this…

The Interview

A 100-word story

Ava needed this job.

With her sister working lates, if Ava landed a day job, their brother could stay with the girls. Together they'd make it work.

"How fast can you type?" asked the interviewer.

"60 words per minute," Ava replied, "75 on an electric."

"Can you work a switchboard?"

"Yes," Ava lied. She'd seen a switchboard at Sears, how hard could it be?

"Do you drive?"

"Yes," again Ava lied. She would catch rides and hitchhike if she had to.

Holding onto the tiny cross, Ava prayed one word, *please*.

The interviewer sighed, "I'll see you in the morning."

He Met His Match

A 100-word story including the word "conference"

"See you after the conference," Sam called as Francine dashed out for her run.

But Francine wasn't running today; she was racing Sam to the conference hotel. *Won't he be surprised,* she thought smugly.

The bartender set a drink next to Francine, winked, then asked, "Waiting for Sam?"

But the woman next to Francine replied, "Yes, he'll be here shortly."

Francine turned to the woman, then looked past her, straight at Sam.

The woman turned toward Francine's husband in time to see his jaw drop, and his face go ghostly white.

Francine and *her* bartender were the only ones smiling.

5.

Dark and Disturbing

These pieces of flash fiction tell tales of a dark side of life and family.

Unsettling moments, difficult choices, and eerie situations can make an intriguing story, even in just a few words.

Mama's Promise

A 100-word story including the word "necessary"

"That liar," I cried into Mama's arms, "I thought we were friends."

Mama stroked my hair while I sobbed, "I'm upset with him, but my hatred for her is worse. I'll never forgive her, never."

"It's not necessary, honey."

"What do you mean, Mama?" I sobbed.

"When a snake bites, do you forgive the snake?"

"No, it's his nature," I replied, "it wouldn't ask forgiveness even if it could."

"She won't ask either," Mama promised.

"How could you know?"

Then, the newscaster's voice cut in, "The body of a 25-year-old woman washed ashore this morning…"

"That's how I know, honey."

The Thin Line

A 100-word story including the word "inches"

Margo beamed as her granddaughter crossed the stage.

Lily's graduation and 18th birthday coincided, and they had one last hurdle: graduation dinner.

Lily's mother, seated beside Margo, leaned toward her mother-in-law and quietly said, "I've sensed that you don't love me anymore."

Margo, her lips inches from Gretch's ear, whispered, "There's a thin line between love and hate. What you previously sensed was for the child's sake, and she's no longer a child."

Lily peeked into her grandmother's purse. Two plane tickets, as promised, and she stifled a cheer!

Eighteen years of Gretch was enough.

Today, they were finally free.

The Psychic and the Stone

A 100-word story using the word "foretell"

The psychic seemed convinced she would foretell my future, and today marked my new beginning.

I was skeptical — that could mean anything.

On my shortcut through the graveyard, a stone appeared out of thin air, I almost ran into it. The print was faint but unmistakable: Sal Heck died on June 9, 2024.

That's today! I reached out to touch it but it vanished.

I sprinted home and found Mother staring out the window.

"Are you alright, mama?" I cried, "Where's Sal?"

"He's gone, honey," she whispered, "He was found dead this morning."

We embraced and cried tears of joy.

The Scrawled Note

A 100-word story, including the word "muddy"

Becky's lungs burned from running. She had ached for a breather; now crouched behind an old tree stump, she waited.

Becky had known for years this day would come. Her past finally caught up with her and today she vowed only one of them would survive the night.

The scrawled note Max handed her during the festivities read: *If I can't have you, he can't either.*

Becky was weary of running, she'd finally face him.

The underbrush rustled, he was near.

Becky ripped the muddy hem of her wedding dress and gently freed the razor-sharp fillet knife.

She came prepared.

The Secret

A 150-word story using the word "skewer"

Nurse Pam sifted through the boxes she had stored in Aunt Ruth's locker.

Ten years' worth of cookware, linens, and odds and ends had to be downsized before Pam relocated overseas for her new job.

"Before I donate anything, do you need this mixing bowl set? Maybe a cutting board?"

"No, I have all I need, honey," Ruth replied.

"Wait, what's this?" Pam asked.

She slid a single 12-inch steel skewer from inside an oven mitt where it had been hidden.

When Pam looked at the dried blood, she froze. Realization dawned as their eyes met.

"He was horrid to you, Aunt Ruth," Pam said quietly, "and he deserved what he got."

"Yes, he was," Ruth replied.

"This secret will go with me to my grave," whispered Pam.

"It's safe with me, too," said Aunt Ruth.

She smiled slightly, "but you already knew that, didn't you?"

Pam nodded. "Thanks, Auntie."

6.

Love and Devotion

Stories of love in all its forms—tender, loyal, passionate, and sometimes messy.

These short pieces capture what it means to open your heart, hold someone close,

and not let go.

The Vow She Kept

A 100-word story using the word "liaison"

Weary of old ways and pious stodgy elders who ruled through fear, Megan vowed she would be free by today. She was done pretending and loved who she was.

Megan spotted Bobbi crossing the street, and when their eyes locked, Bobbi smiled seductively.

As Megan slowly crossed her slender, long legs, one shoe slipped off.

Megan's attempts at being alluring always became comedic, but when Bobbi's smile transformed into pure adoration, Megan knew she had found her soulmate.

What started as a liaison had deepened; this beautiful love confirmed to Megan that her hard-won struggle for freedom was completely worthwhile.

What The Dog Really Thinks of Hiking

A 100-word story

Patricia and I (the dog) admired the view from the top, then she plotted our route down to the canyon floor.

"This should be no problem," Patricia said optimistically, "look Cooper, it's downhill all the way!"

What? Ok Captain Obvious, I thought, *and I know who will need a snack before we start our trek down.*

Once we arrive in the valley, Pat will buckle up my harness, I'll hold out for more snacks and mentally prepare for our hike back up.

It's a good thing I love hauling, and I love her, so sure, I can call it *hiking*.

My Birthday Toast

A 100-word story using the word "toast"

"Hey Buddy, how did your feet get soaked?" Cooper asked.

"The forest floor was damp with last night's rain," Buddy replied.

"Why were you in the forest?"

"Gathering wildflowers for the lady's birthday."

"You're sensitive deep down, Bud."

"What will you give her, Cooper?"

"I'll prepare the toast."

"Toast?" both cats looked dubious.

"Yes, people get toast for special occasions. But I might knock things off the counter," Cooper said, "Will you pop the bread in the toaster, Zoey?"

"Sure, and I'll arrange tea and marmalade, too."

"This is the best birthday ever!" the lady said, brushing away a tear.

Would I Be Lost Without You?

A 100-word poem

I ran out of coffee, put salt in my tea,
and matched my blue shirt with a skirt colored
green.

I hopped on the wrong bus and went in
the *out* door. I stepped off the elevator on the
wrong floor.

You're under the weather, you've got the day
off, and I'm on my own while they tend to your
cough.

You're probably bored, so get better real quick.
Let's get back to normal, I am lost when you're
sick.

We'll walk in the morning, so get lots of rest,
today I feel scattered but with you, life's the
best.

7.

Buddy's Bravado

Buddy, the confident, street-smart cat is certain he's the cleverest creature in any room.

He's a self-proclaimed master hunter, a feline philosopher, and occasionally, a softie when it comes to Cooper and even Zoey… though he'd never admit it outright.

Chicks Adored Buddy

A 150-word flash fiction story using the word "model"

"Hey Cooper," Buddy asked casually, "See that kitten on the sidewalk?"

"I do; he's pretty adorable as kittens go."

"That's a model kitten who will grow into a model citizen in the cat community; mark my words."

"How are you defining model, Bud?" Cooper asked.

"First, he's handsome. He'll have a good dose of arrogance and will be clever, naturally.

"He'll love lasagna like Garfield on a Monday.

"He'll adopt a home with a dog and humans who'll feed and care for him and appreciate his awesomeness."

"How can you be so sure?" Cooper asked.

"Before I moved in here, I was the alley boss, and chicks—uhh, cats—adored me.

"I drove them insane; I was their catnip."

"I'm sure you were," Cooper nodded.

"Also," Buddy boasted, "I am all of the above, and that cute kitten is my offspring."

"I never would have doubted it," Cooper agreed.

Buddy's Piece of Trivia

A 125-word flash fiction story using the word "viaduct"

"Hey Cooper, how about a piece of trivia?" Buddy asked casually.

"Sure!" Cooper replied, "As long as there's ketchup. I don't trust mystery meat."

"Trivia's not meat, and what is *mystery* meat?"

"Nobody knows," Cooper replied, "that's why they call it mystery meat."

"Good point," Buddy nodded.

Zoey chimed in, "What's the trivia already?"

Buddy blinked and returned to the topic, "Did you know we live a stone's throw from the largest railway structure of its kind in the world? The Lethbridge Viaduct, completed in 1909; it's still used and maintained today."

"Why do we need this information?" Zoey asked.

"We don't, that's why it's called trivia." Cooper said, walking toward the fridge, "I'm ready for a piece of actual meat; are you guys hungry?"

A Delicious New Dish, or Lasagna?

A 100-word story with the word "marketing"

"I'm feeling light and springy today," Zoey mewed cheerily.

"Have you been sneaking coffee again?" Buddy asked.

"Not today; I just had a lovely dish of food that's supposed to make cats feel light on their feet."

"Ah, the clever marketing ploy. Light on their feet is the new way to say it's diet food," Buddy grumbled. "Frankly, I feel like I fell off the edge of the earth."

Cooper chimed in, "That was the edge of the couch, Bud. Could it be that lasagna the lady left unattended?"

"Cooper, my good man, lasagna helps supplement my reduced calorie intake."

The Crossroads

A 100-word story with the word "desire"

The road ahead was closed.

Lady: Our choices are left for burgers, right for chicken, or backtrack for pizza.

Buddy: Backtrack, pizza is my heart's desire.

Zoey: I vote for chicken.

Cooper: Are there fries with the chicken?

Zoey: Dogs can't have fries.

Cooper: I've had fries before and I'm fine.

Buddy: No one saw it.

Cooper: I'm smart Bud, I wait till the lady walks away.

Buddy: She's sitting right here.

Cooper: No problem, she'll walk away again.

Buddy: Next time she'll take her fries.

Zoey: Guys, hello! She talks to us but she doesn't hear us.

Buddy: Obviously.

The Pets Discuss a Yoga Move

A 100-word story using the word "school"

Zoey: I took a class.

Buddy: You mean like, school?

Zoey: No, I watched a Yoga class on YouTube with the lady; they taught stretches.

Cooper: There's a Yoga move they got from dogs.

Buddy: Indeed, the downward dog.

Zoey: That's a move?

Cooper: Yes, it's to limber up after resting.

Zoey: Can cats do it?

Buddy: We already do, you didn't need a class.

Zoey: The downward dog is a stretch?

Cooper: No, it's a move.

Buddy: A stretch is a move, guys.

Cooper: I'm sure I knew that.

Buddy: You're smarter than you think, Cooper.

Zoey looks confused.

8.

Humorous, Even Silly

These stories are full of quirky moments,
twists, and a bit of nonsense.

They're meant to make you smile, and maybe
even laugh out loud.

He Knew Exactly What She Meant

A 100-word story using the word "size"

"It's not the right size for you, hon?" he asked.

"No, too short," she replied.

"I'm sure it will reach those lovely petunias of yours."

"If I pull on it, maybe. But I don't want to pound my petunias either, do you know what I mean?"

"Yes, exactly."

"Let's try extending it as far as it will stretch."

"Good idea! You should have the best tools for times when I can't be there."

"You're so thoughtful but enough talking. Let's do this."

"Alrighty," he smiled and grabbing the green 50-footer, "this hose should reach your petunias plus the entire garden."

Going Out to Pick Up Something

A 100-word story using the word "shizizle"

"Where are you going?"

"Outside."

"Why?"

"To pick up shizizle."

"Who's that?"

"It's a what."

"What?"

"What's that, not who."

"What's what?"

"Shizizle."

"Bless you."

"I didn't sneeze."

"I'm calling your therapist."

"I don't have a therapist."

"I'll find one for you."

"Why?"

"You're not making sense."

"Who me? How?"

"You're picking up who? But who's a what, and right there's where you lost me."

"Where?"

(confused silence)

"Why are you taking the dog?"

"So he can do his business, then I'll pick up the shizizzle. Do I need to spell it out?"

"Yes, please."

"It's s-h-i-t, hon."

"Shizizzle's shit?"

To-Do List Catastrophe

A 100-word story

One year ago, I made a To-Do list for the new year.

My first item was to do one push up from floor level.

The worst part about this grueling exercise is, in the *up* position, I start laughing.

My arms are so long that from the top, I foresee a faceplant.

To make matters worse, I planned to add one every few weeks, so by year-end, I'd be doing at least three push ups.

On the subject of To-Do lists, my 2024 exercise routine will begin when I have a yoga mat, you know, for a softer landing.

The Best Day of Leap Year is Feb 29

A 100-word story using the word "assistant"

We lament about time, saying *if only I had one extra day.*

Today's that day!

On this Leap Day 2024, I'll need an assistant for the things I've saved for today.

There's a closet to organize and a spare room to dust. I need to sort the child's toys into *too babyish* and *currently playing with.*

I want to make a chocolate pie with extra shredded chocolate and a buttery graham crumb crust.

And here's the best thing about Leap Day — calories don't count, and if you've been around since 1924, you're 24.

Happy Birthday to Leap Year babies everywhere!

9.

Layla's Story of Love and Loss

In these flash fiction snapshots, Layla is caught between passion, escape, and the pull of freedom.

The Kiss

A 100-word story using the word "frame"

Their warm private booth felt close, but red wine eased the tension.

He pulled Layla to him. His mouth found hers, searching for the connection they craved.

Passion gripped them, and Layla felt that familiar tightening at her core.

Her brain shouted, *fight this, he's good!*

How she detested that frame of mind — her conscience — an incessant killjoy.

Layla tried to slow her racing heart, but the smoky heat of his neck was unbearable.

She smelled his blood, and she needed desperately, to sink her teeth into his delicious skin.

Stopping now would be torturous, but to keep going — deadly.

The Violet Sapphire

A 100-word story

Layla had stashed enough money, she could go anywhere, but she was torn.

One man had haunted her dreams.

He said he wanted to know her, deeply, all of her, and called her his violet sapphire.

She'd asked why, and remembered his lips brush her neck as he had whispered, *they are as rare and beautiful as you*.

She still felt the churning at her core, this marked a crossroads — she must determine whether to stay and be with him or take her passport and continue her journey.

She'd go where she could blend in, and start over, yet again.

Love Letter

A 100-word story

Her bags were packed; Layla was ready to go. She slid a sheet of paper from the drawer and began writing:

Dearest Edward,
I've loved you since you called me your violet sapphire.
Every night, I hear your voice and feel your warm lips on my skin.
But I need an honest life—I can't keep looking over my shoulder.
I'm going back to my music. I'll contact you when the time is right.
Yours always, Layla

The taxi waited. She'd mail the letter at the airport.
A single tear slipped down her cheek and landed on the word *loved*.

Is Freedom Just Her Illusion?

A 100-word story

Layla waited at Gate 45—ten minutes until departure.

Edward would receive her letter in a few days; she'd be in Sydney by then.

Her phone buzzed. The screen flashed: *Him*, but she pressed *Decline*. Would she regret it?

Her heart pounded in her ears, and she took deep breaths to keep from throwing up.

It rang again. *Him*.

She hesitated, then answered. "Edward?"

"Layla! Don't hang up. You're at the airport?"

"How did you know?"

"I hear planes in the background."

She rolled her eyes at herself.

"Layla, wait, I'll—"

Boarding began.

"I'm sorry."
She ended the call.

10.

I'll Wrap it up Here

With one personal story and one a bit lighter,
I'll end my little book of flash fiction.

Thank you for taking time to read my serious,
dark, and humorous discussions
among the pets.

Each story was a pleasure to write, and I hope
you found them enjoyable to read!

Listen and See

A 100-word story using the word "listen"

Today, I'm going to the woods

In the woods, I hear more than I see, and
I see more when I listen.

Before I stop to listen, I see colors of the sky
and earth-tones of the forest.

But when I listen, I hear wildlife calling out
warnings,

a human is present.

Leaves rustle in time to the breeze,

small branches snap,

large boughs sway to create unique low tones.

Woodland creatures skitter through
undergrowth,

Their warnings change to sounds of curiosity

the longer I remain quiet, and present.

Today, I'm going to the woods,

I'll experience a natural symphony.

Come Skydiving With Me?

A 100-word story using the word "insidious"

"Can you use *insidiou*s in a sentence?" asked the wife.

"Your humor is insidious," the husband replied.

"How is my humor insidious?"

"It's subtle and treacherous."

"I just asked if you would go skydiving with me."

"Exactly! I dread heights. You'd have to trick me into putting on a parachute, then lure me into the helicopter.

"Someone would have to push me out… why are you laughing?"

"A helicopter, wouldn't that be tempting fate?"

"No, don't forget, gravity… why are you still laughing?"

"I'm imagining someone tangled in a ceiling fan."

"You confirm my point. Your humor is insidious."

www.ingramcontent.com/pod-product-compliance
Lightning Source LLC
Chambersburg PA
CBHW071832020426
42331CB00007B/1702

Daniel Orr's

Latin for the Zombie Apocalypse

A.K.A.

"In Case You Need To Talk To The Dead (Romans)."

"Completely Dead Language for Fun with the dead"

To my daughters,

   Just in case you ever get thrust back in time or if there are Etruscans during the zombie apocalypse.

Dedicated to:

Freya Brighton, Haley Rae
Faith Alexis, Lara Danielle

Disclaimer: This text may not prevent you from being eaten by zombies nor help you in a court. Courtrooms are nearly the same thing as a zombie apocalypse (hopeless situation). The author has never actually met a Roman or a Zombie but lawyers and judges provided essential inspirations since they are known to eat you alive. The author does not swear by any pronunciations but it is true (as of this writing) that no dead Roman has ever sent me an email to complain or correct me.

Pirates are better than ninjas.

Also, pirates are cooler than ninjas.
